Dear Rose & Gary

In my book, you are not only heroes, but good friends! How lucky I am!

Your presence & your example have taught me more than you can imagine, and I'm very grateful for all I have learned from you!

Congratulations on your 50th Anniversary!

May you be blessed with many more healthy, happy and peace-filled years together!

Love,
S. Marie

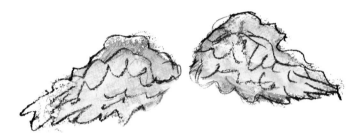

To my Uncle Jack, my first hero;

and to my son, Rick, who was born a hero.

— Flavia

To Mark,

whose heroic heart breathes life into my soul,

and whose very existence makes me thankful

to be a part of the human race;

and to my beloved Sylvie,

the most courageous spirit of all.

— Lisa

ordinary HEROES

WRITTEN BY FLAVIA AND LISA WEEDN

ILLUSTRATED BY FLAVIA WEEDN

THE WORLD
KNOWS LITTLE OF
ITS GREATEST HEROES.

GREATNESS

Heroes walk among us.

They appear without

a sign, a voice, or

a sound to rescue

those in need.

From very near or

very far away, they

come to comfort,

protect, and touch

the lives of known

or unknown

names and faces.

Who they are,

their actions,

their dedication,

and their

accomplishments

are seldom

printed on

any page…

...not heralded

on television,

or honored

on the radio;

sometimes,

they aren't even

noted at all.

HEAVEN SMILES SOFTLY
AND HEARS EVERY WISH.

Heroes ask

for no reward

or fanfare.

They bring

their gifts

because they have

a higher calling,

a sense of purpose

from above.

heart

The hero's heart

listens to the

hearts of others

and responds.

Heroes warm the cold,

soothe the hurt,

and feed the soul

simply because

they care enough.

COMPASSION

TELL ME OF YOUR HURT.
I AM HERE AND
MY HEART WILL LISTEN.

With truth and

inner beauty

as their guides,

heroes do what

they must do,

go where they must go,

propelled only by the

voice of their spirit

and the heartbeat

of their soul.

*Courage makes a hero

reach for a comrade's hand

in a city street or on

a distant battlefield.

Faith makes a hero

venture into the

dark and unknown.

Dedication, duty,

and the strength

of their convictions

make heroes

defend us for as long

a time as needed.*

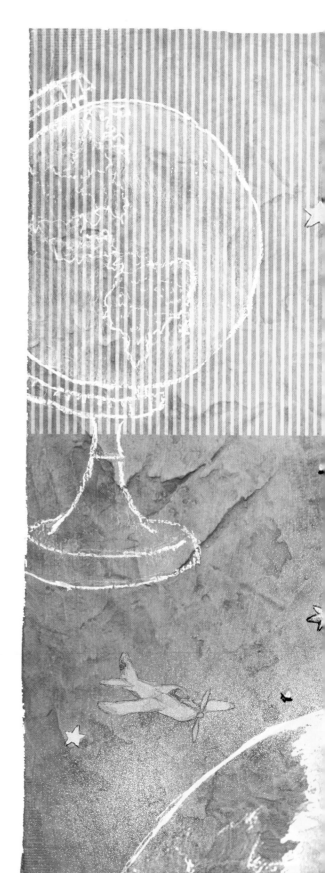

Our heroes

face the world

and are able

to continue on

when their bodies

are more than tired,

because their

spirits will not

let them take rest.

*T*hese are

the quiet heroes,

those who have

no need of

a clock to tell

them when

it's time to quit.

IF I COULD SIT ACROSS THE PORCH FROM GOD,
I'D THANK HIM FOR LENDING ME YOU.

Great heroes are found

not only at battle

or at war. Some are

right here with us

and are a part of

our everyday lives.

They help us feel safe

and give us strength

by letting us know

they are near.

faith

Ordinary heroes

may not be trained,

hold titles,

or carry badges.

Sometimes ordinary

heroes are born

in an instant,

by making a decision

when the need

is clear and faith

is stronger than fear.

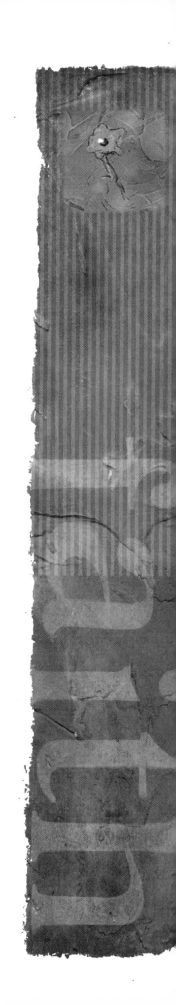

SPIRIT

TIME HAS NO MEANING

IN MATTERS OF THE HEART.

Without a

blare of trumpets

or a cheering crowd,

an ordinary hero

steps forth.

Such heroes will

take action simply

because they know

the difference

that a minute,

or even a second,

can make.

HOPE

ANGELS ARE ALL AROUND US,
AND ANY HEART WHO YEARNS TO
CAN REACH OUT AND TOUCH A WING.

Ordinary heroes

are most often humble.

They rarely know

they are akin to angels,

and that the song

of their spirits

will live forever.

kindness

CARE

A HAND
TO HOLD

Some heroes are

our neighbors,

faces we see everyday.

They are a part

of our community,

our chosen circle.

They greet us with

familiar gestures,

improving our

journey in ways

we may never

know or see.

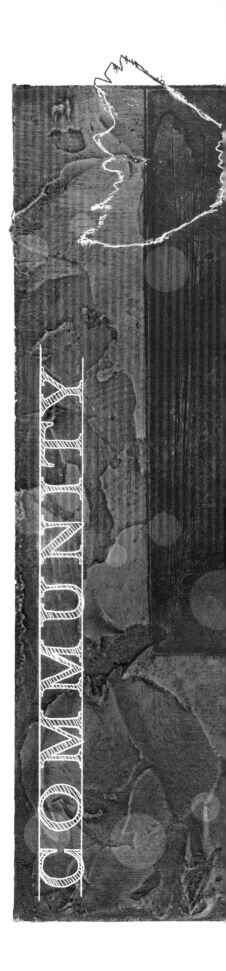

In every ordinary day there are a thousand MIRACLES.

An ordinary hero

can be someone

in our family,

one who shares

our story and

understands

who we really

are inside.

A hero can be

someone with

whom we work,

or a stranger on

an elevator, a bus,

or an airplane.

The greatest heroes

can be anywhere and

everywhere we are.

We know heroes

by the light they cast.

Their shimmering

presence may walk

beside us for a while,

or pass through us quickly.

No matter how long

their stay, their guidance

brightens our lives

and leaves a mark

on us forever.

BRIGHT
SPIRIT

FRIENDSHIP

FRIENDS TAKE US
BY THE HAND
AND HELP US TO KNOW
WE ARE NEVER ALONE.

Heroes are friends

who greet us with a smile,

extend their joy,

and listen to our

disappointments

and dreams without

being critical of either.

They are attentive

companions who make

the time to laugh

and cry and care.

KINDNESS

WE are each
a part of ALL
THAT SURROUNDS US.

A hero can be a passerby

or a shopkeeper who is

free with a compliment,

one who is willing

to share kindness

when we need so much

to hear kind words.

Such heroes lift us up

and give us reason

to believe that

we are part of a

much greater whole.

Ordinary heroes

are those who put

the innocent first,

who take away

the hurt and

bring a smile

where there was

none before.

IT IS WISDOM
TO REACH FOR A HAND
THAT NEEDS YOU.

GENTLENESS

Some are strong

and brave mothers

who face the world alone,

yet still manage

to understand

a child's secret grief

and soothe away

hidden tears.

MOTHERHOOD

CARE

COMPASSION

GRACE

TENDERNESS

Hearts

Some heroes are

mothers who teach us

the importance

of having faith in

ourselves, encourage

us to let our spirits

dance, and show us

how to believe

in our dreams

no matter where

or how we live.

They know it is

more important

to teach a child

how love can

live forever,

than it is to

force the child's

understanding

during times when

understanding

is the hardest

thing of all.

PROTECT

HONOR

LISTEN

LOVE

Ordinary heroes

are fathers

who keep

their promises,

whose words

a child can trust.

protect

Ordinary heroes

are dads who comfort us

when we're afraid,

who put aside

other things just

to spend time with us,

who tell us they

enjoy being with us,

and mean it.

They are fathers

who show us right

from wrong with

humor and patience,

and let us know

we are loved

no matter what.

Heroes are

there for us

and will listen

because they know

that whatever

we need to say

needs to be heard.

LISTENING HEART

EVERY VOICE
NEEDS TO
BE HEARD.

"AND WHAT IS AS IMPORTANT
AS KNOWLEDGE?" ASKED THE MIND.
"CARING AND SEEING WITH THE HEART,"
ANSWERED THE SOUL.

SOUL

IMPORTANCE

Heroes mend

broken toys as well

as broken hearts.

They ease simple

burdens, aware

that burdens

are never simple

to those who

carry them.

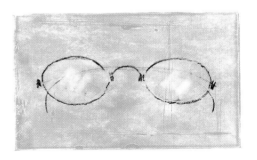

Heroes defend the honor of children and stand up for their rights. They show them how faith and hope live within their hearts, and as long as they believe, their dreams will never die.

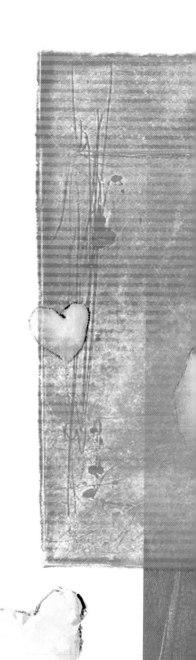

Some heroes

are teachers who

unveil the universe

to our minds,

teach us to read,

speak in languages

other than our own,

and give us knowledge

that becomes strength.

They speak

of those who

have lived before,

so we'll know

of where we've come.

They help us

understand that

we belong and that

every one of us matters.

KNOWLEDGE

EXPANDING OUR MINDS

SHOWS US HOW TO MAKE OUR WORLD

A GOOD AND BETTER PLACE.

future

Some heroes

bring technology

to prepare us

for the changing

world of tomorrow.

They give us hope

for the future in which

our children will live.

Some teach tolerance

and how to accept others

for who they are and

not what we think

they might be or

wish they were.

They show us that

judgment blinds us

to the truth, and that

it is only through

the eyes of compassion

that we are able to truly see.

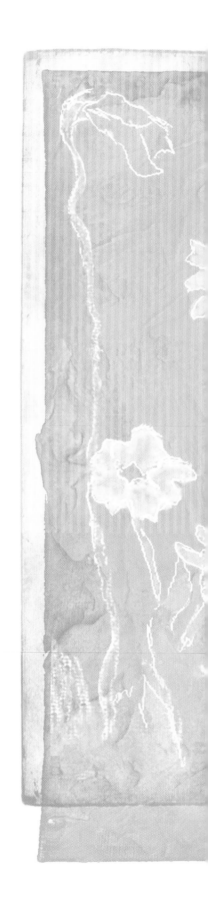

EQUALITY

ACCEPTANCE TEACHES US
THAT WE ARE EACH
DIFFERENT IN SOME WAY
AND EQUAL IN ALL WAYS.

Some heroes

are coaches who

champion physical

abilities and teach us

the importance

of teamwork

and fairness,

and in so doing so,

strengthen our

bodies and minds.

WITHIN EACH OF US
THERE LIVES THE STRENGTH
OF A CHAMPION.

RESPECT

IT IS NEVER EASY
REACHING FOR DREAMS,
BUT THOSE WHO REACH
WALK IN STARDUST.

VISION

*T*hey polish our

skills and give us

the courage

to strive for

goals higher

than we ever

thought we

could reach.

Ordinary heroes

are our mentors,

our role models.

They show us

we can overcome

anything and be

all we yearn to be

if we keep growing

and never give up.

They are heroes who,

not with words

but by example,

show us

the right

and fair way

to treat ourselves

and others.

THE HERO'S HEART WITHIN US
ALWAYS FINDS ITS WAY HOME.

PURPOSE

They redirect us
when we are lost
and help us
to help ourselves
find the right
path home.

They show us

the way to be

content and

at peace when

we're alone

with our thoughts.

These heroes

teach us character.

MERCY

CHARACTER

CONTEMPLATION

PRAYER

Ordinary heroes

are often unaware

they are setting

an example.

By the way

they live their

own lives, they

change the course

of other lives,

making a

difference forever.

CHANGE

To BELIEVE is to know that
life is a series of new beginnings.

Heroes are those

who let it be known

that no one

is ever a failure,

and that to be

a true success means

to have the courage

to pick up the pieces

when it's time

to begin again.

Heroes experience

life deeply.

They conquer fear

by embracing

each moment,

and their freedom

to be right here,

right now.

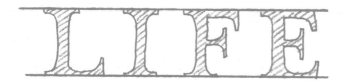

LIFE IS BRIEF.
FOLLOW YOUR HEART.

Heroes are moved

to share. They are

unashamed to feel.

They expose their

hearts in their

words, art, and music,

so that others may

benefit from

their expression.

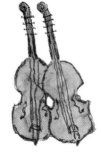

UNITY

WE ARE ALL FAMILY

IN THIS JOURNEY OF LIFE.

family

With an impassioned

stroke of creative

genius, they craft

works of the soul

that inspire unity,

connect beauty with

a message of hope,

and allow those whom

they have never met

feel they are not alone.

With their strength
of purpose and
a thirst for truth,
they move beyond
traditional logic.
With their
passionate will,
they create ideas
that can change the
course of humanity.

LIFE

miracle

A PASSION FOR LIFE
CANNOT BE PUT OUT.
ITS LIGHT INSPIRES
POSITIVE CHANGE.

PASSION

Heroes are those

who have learned

that by experiencing

life's heartaches

we all come to know

the importance

of tenderness...

...and that in the echo

of broken dreams

the human instinct

for compassion

will come forward,

welcoming those

who need its blessing.

HEROES

A HERO IS SOMEONE
WHO **BELIEVES** IN US
AND WORKS WITH US
TO REALIZE OUR **DREAMS.**

Ordinary heroes

show us that

real joy

can be found

in dreaming,

for they know

that having

a dream is

as necessary to

the heart as love.

Our soul mates,

spouses and lovers,

and all others

who make us want

to love better and

love more, are

our real heroes.

For love is the

lamp that lights

our way.

LOVE

LOVE
IS WHAT
MATTERS
MOST.

SOUL

KEEP

LOVE

INSPIRE

LIFE'S LANDSCAPE IS LARGER

THAN WE CAN SEE.

BEYOND THE **HORIZON,**

TOMORROW AWAITS OUR TOUCH.

Heroes inspire us.

They open our minds

to the larger landscape

of life. They help us

to see who we are and

who we may someday

become. They show

us that every ordinary

day is filled with

extraordinary surprises.

CARE

TRUST

COMMITMENT

QUALITY

HUMAN SPIRIT

Caregivers, doctors,

and nurses are

often heroes,

sharing not only their

skill and knowledge,

but also lending us a

caring shoulder.

They make a profound

difference in the quality

of our lives and the

lives of those we love.

Heroes soothe

not only our

everyday worries,

but also offer comfort

and compassion

when we need it most.

They invite our trust,

and know when to

give of themselves

in hundreds of

ordinary ways.

COMFORT

I WISH I COULD
TAKE AWAY THE HURT.

Many heroes work

behind the scenes

to sustain our lives

and protect our world.

They know that

great things come

from a series

of small actions.

These heroes recognize

a need and fill it.

They provide aid,

shelter, and support,

working tirelessly

to be a voice for

those who have none.

HEART

LAND

OF THE

BRAVE

Heroes are the brave,

armed with vision

and conviction.

They protect and

defend so that

others may live.

They are steadfast

in their mission.

Their values are

never for sale.

*T*hese are

the heroes with

hearts that dare;

the seemingly

ordinary men

and women

whose guiding

desire is to

give more than

they take.

GIVE WHAT
YOU HAVE.
DARE TO LOVE
WITH ABANDON.

Heroes are not

afraid of life.

They embrace it.

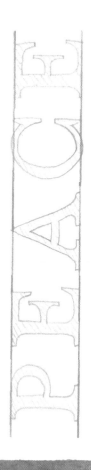

*T*hey cherish

the privilege

of being alive

and sharing this

time on earth.

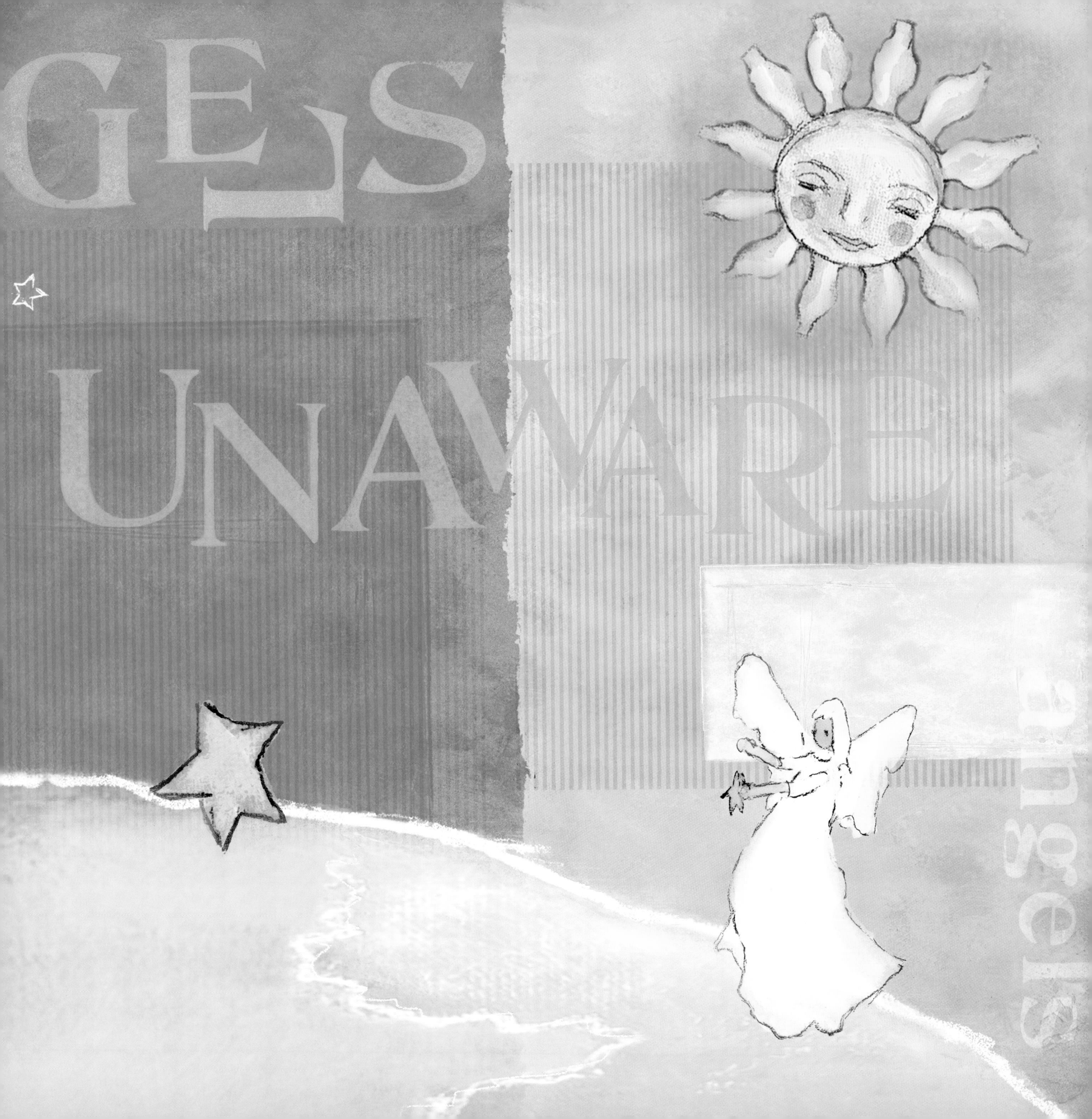
GELS
UNAWARE
angels

Heroes are often

ordinary people

whose lives don't

look much different

than our own.

Yet within each

of them is a

champion for humanity,

for the well-being

of our country, and

for peace in the world.

Some heroes

wear uniforms,

some do not.

But the armor

each of them wears

is built of integrity,

mercy, and love.

The power of such a

shield can never be

pierced or broken.

INTEGRITY

SOME PEOPLE LIVE IN
OUR HEARTS FOREVER.

GRATITUDE

HEROES ARE MESSENGERS
FROM HEAVEN.
THEIR LOVE IS GOD'S
TOUCH ON HUMANITY.

life

High thanks we owe

to those who have

protected us from harm,

who have mended our

spirits and given us

faith to carry on.

Though they ask for

nothing in return, let our

gratitude be outspoken,

for life is too fleeting

and far too fragile to

let words go unsaid.

In honor of those

who have come

before us,

may we always

reach out to those

in need, and may

the circle of life

inspire us

to give back

for all that we've

been given.

May we embrace

the hope that

within each of us

there lives an

ordinary hero,

for the divine

capacity of the

human spirit

can make us all

angels unaware.

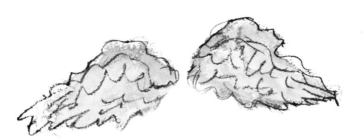

ISBN 0-7683-2570-6

WRITTEN BY FLAVIA AND LISA WEEDN
ILLUSTRATED BY FLAVIA WEEDN
© WEEDN FAMILY TRUST
WWW.FLAVIA.COM
ALL RIGHTS RESERVED

PUBLISHED IN 2003 BY CEDCO PUBLISHING COMPANY
100 PELICAN WAY, SAN RAFAEL, CALIFORNIA 94901
FOR A FREE CATALOG OF OTHER CEDCO® PRODUCTS, PLEASE WRITE
TO THE ADDRESS ABOVE, OR VISIT OUR WEBSITE: WWW.CEDCO.COM

PRINTED IN SPAIN
1 3 5 7 9 10 8 6 4 2

THE ARTWORK FOR EACH PICTURE IS DIGITALLY MASTERED USING ACRYLIC ON CANVAS.

WITH LOVE AND GRATITUDE TO OUR HEROES—RICK, SYLVIE, LISA, LARRY, MATHIEU, MATT, DIANA, AMBER, PAUL, SERAPHIM, BARBARA, SUE, MARK, WARREN, JARROD, SAM, CORY, JANE, TYLER, HUI-YING TING, BRIAN, ANNA, JANICE AND LAURA